# 1    Introduction

Retail distribution is a requirement for retail sales. One would therefore expect demand studies to account for product availability in a careful manner. In practice, however, the role of retail distribution is implicitly determined by the level of data aggregation employed. Demand studies based on store-level data typically assume consumers limit their purchases to products available at a particular store. Previous research suggests this is a reasonable approximation for certain types of goods, such as grocery products (Rhee and Bell 2002). This highlights a potential problem in demand analyses that use regionally or nationally aggregated data, since they make the opposite assumption.[1] Such studies assume consumers freely choose between all products available in a given market, even items carried by very few stores. They ignore search and transportation costs that may lead consumers to limit their choice sets to a subset of the available items.

The following example illustrates why this approach is potentially problematic. In 2000, the Federal Trade Commission (FTC) challenged the acquisition of Beech-Nut Nutrition Corporation by H.J. Heinz Company, both manufacturers of baby food. The district court judge noted that "nearly all supermarkets stock only two brands of baby food, not three…Gerber is invariably one of the two."[2] The fraction of stores that carried Gerber, Heinz, and Beech-Nut was approximately 100%, 40%, and 45%, respectively.[3] Standard aggregate demand models would fail to control for this distribution pattern if consumers primarily substitute between products available at the same store. One would expect estimated cross-price elasticities between Heinz and Beech-Nut to be close to zero not because consumers are necessarily unwilling to substitute between them, but because few consumers visit stores where both are available.

---

[1] Throughout the paper, "aggregate data" refers to when sales from multiple stores are combined.

[2] *FTC v. H. J. Heinz Co.*, 116 F. Supp. 2d (D.D.C. 2000) at 193.

[3] *Id.* at 194.

Our objective is to measure how frequently this problem occurs. The relevant issue is not *whether* a product is available, but rather *to what extent* it is available. Looking at five grocery categories, we show that far more products have limited distribution than one might expect given how little attention this issue has received in the demand estimation literature. While the baby food example is atypical, our results suggest that a more subtle form of this problem commonly occurs. Through Monte Carlo analysis, we show that typical levels of limited product availability can significantly bias the results of aggregate demand models that ignore product assortment heterogeneity across stores.

We conclude by exploring why products have limited retail distribution. As expected, many such items are niche products with de minimus sales. However, products with intermediate levels of retail distribution account for approximately 25% of total sales, which is a non-trivial amount.[4] We highlight several reasons why this is the case. First, even though stores generally carry the same product lines, they select different assortments of product varieties from them. Second, it often takes many weeks for a retail-chain to introduce a new item across its stores. Lastly, even top-selling items have occasional stock-outs.

The paper is organized as follows. Section 2 reviews the literature on retail distribution and discusses how demand studies account for product availability. Section 3 describes the dataset employed. Section 4 demonstrates that many products have limited retail distribution, and section 5 considers the implications of this finding for demand analysis. Section 6 explores why limited product availability occurs. Section 7 concludes.

## 2    Literature Review

Researchers widely recognize the importance of retail distribution. This is most evident in the vertical control literature, where the underlying maxim is that manufacturers require retail

---

[4] We define retail distribution as "intermediate" if a product is available at 50% to 90% of stores. See section 4 for further details.

distribution to sell their products.[5] The search cost literature also highlights the importance of retail distribution. Rhee and Bell (2002) show that, over extended periods of time, consumers make the vast majority of their grocery purchases at a single store. Kumar and Leone (1988), Bucklin and Lattin (1992), and Pesendorfer (2002) look at whether promotions persuade consumers to switch grocery stores. Although there is some evidence of inter-store substitution, these studies suggest that consumers largely restrict their grocery purchases to those items available at a single retailer.

A number of marketing studies explicitly focus on retail distribution. Farris et al. (1989), Reibstein and Farris (1995), and Bronnenberg et al. (2000) analyze the relationship between distribution and market share. Cotterill et al. (2000) do the same for private label products. Olver and Farris (1989) consider distribution in the context of push and pull marketing. Curhan (1972) and Drèze et al. (1994) look at how shelf-space allocation affects sales. Draganska and Jain (2005) consider the impact of product assortment on the demand for yogurt. Stassen et al. (1999) analyze the relationship between product assortment and store choice. Bergen et al. (1996) investigate whether product proliferation within brands leads to higher retail distribution.

Despite widespread appreciation that retail distribution is a necessary precursor for retail sales, product availability plays a surprisingly minor role in demand estimation. One strand of the literature uses store-level data to estimate the demand for individual products (e.g., Besanko et al. 2003, Chintagunta et al. 2003, Gupta et al. 1996, Hoch et al. 1995). These papers assume each consumer visits a single store, and chooses from among the available items. This presumes inter-store substitution is sufficiently small that it can be ignored. A benefit of this modeling approach is that consumer choice sets are readily observed, since a product is either available in a given store, or it is not.

---

[5] Examples include Steiner (1976, 2004) and Villas-Boas (2005) who focus on vertical contracting, while Shaffer (1991) and Sullivan (1997) focus on the specific practice of slotting allowances. Asker (2004a, 2004b), Brenkers and Verboven (2004), Heide et al. (1998), and Ornstein and Hanssens (1987) examine vertical restraints, while Lafontaine (1992), Lafontaine and Slade (1997), and Lafontaine and Shaw (1999) cover franchising.

Many demand studies, however, rely on data aggregated across multiple retail outlets (e.g., all stores in a given city). Examples are Hausman et al. (1994), Hausman and Leonard (2002), Berry et al. (1995), Nevo (2001), and Petrin (2002). These analyses assume that consumer choice sets include all products available in a given market, even if an item is available in only a few stores. The plausibility of this assumption depends on the degree to which stores carry different sets of products. Consumers may be unwilling to search across many stores for a given item, especially if the search area contains hundreds or thousands of stores (which is often the case for regionally or nationally aggregated data).

To summarize, product availability plays a very limited role in demand estimation. Strong assumptions are made regarding the relationship between product availability and consumer choice sets without supporting evidence regarding their plausibility. As illustrated by the baby food example described in the introduction, this approach is problematic when there is significant heterogeneity in product availability across stores. The objective of this paper is to determine whether the degree of limited product availability that typically occurs is sufficient to bias significantly the results of aggregate demand models that incorrectly assume all consumers face the same choice set.

## 3 Data

We utilize weekly scanner data provided by ACNielsen that covers five grocery categories: frozen novelties, shelf-stable pasta, hot dogs, ice cream, and salad dressing. The data reports sales from fourteen retailer-city combinations for the period December 1998 to June 2001 (132 weeks).[6] For each UPC, the dataset reports dollar and unit sales, and the percentage of stores that carry that item. Recognizing that stores significantly vary by size, ACNielsen weights each store by its annual dollar sales (across all product categories) when calculating the percentage of stores where each product is available. This measure, known as "All Commodity

---

[6] A confidentiality agreement with ACNielsen prohibits retailer names from being revealed.

Volume" ("ACV"), is the standard metric that brand managers and other practitioners use to quantify a product's retail distribution.

In addition, the dataset reports the ACV of each product line, which is a collection of similar UPCs from the same brand. For example, "Ben & Jerry's ice cream" and "Ben & Jerry's frozen yogurt" are distinct product lines. A product line's ACV reports the percentage of stores that carry at least one UPC from that line. In section 6, we use this measure to examine whether UPCs with limited retail distribution are secondary varieties or package sizes of widely available product lines.

## 4        The Extent of Retail Distribution

Aggregate demand models consider a product "available" if it is sold in at least one store in a given market, irrespective of how many stores actually carry the particular item. We employ a finer categorization of each product's availability. UPCs carried by less than 50% of stores are defined as having "low availability," items carried in 50% to 90% of stores have "intermediate availability," and products carried by at least 90% of stores have "wide availability." Since a product's availability changes over time, we categorize each UPC based on its median retail distribution (although in subsequent analysis we consider intertemporal variation in product availability). To make our definition comparable to how product availability is defined in aggregate demand models, this calculation is separately undertaken for each retailer-city combination. That is, the same UPC in a different retailer-city is treated as a distinct product.

Table 1 reports the percentage of products and dollar sales represented by each of these groups. Widely available products generally comprise less than one quarter of all items. The only exception is hot dogs, but even in that category, only 41% of products are widely available. Our finding that most products are not widely available may come as a surprise. Prior to analyzing the data, the impression from our own shopping experiences was that most items are available "everywhere." While clearly not true, this perception is likely due to the finding, also from Table 1, that a majority of each category's sales is derived from a small set of products that are widely available. Depending on the category, 62% to 81% of dollar sales come from products with a median retail distribution of at least 90% of stores.

Our findings indicate that while supermarket chains carry a fairly homogeneous set of popular items (i.e., widely available, top-selling items), stores have different assortments of low-selling products. To simplify the analysis, researchers commonly exclude low-selling items when estimating demand (e.g., Chintagunta 2002, Nevo and Hatzitaskos 2005). The fact that low-selling items often have low product availability is obviously immaterial when such products are excluded from the data sample.

However, a third set of products with intermediate distribution does pose a problem for demand estimation. Unlike products with low availability, this set of items constitutes a substantial fraction of dollar sales, 16% to 33% depending on the product category. Moreover, they constitute between 19% and 43% of all available products. Items with intermediate product availability are too numerous and too large a fraction of total sales to be reasonably ignored in demand analyses. However, since such products are not carried by a significant fraction of stores, inclusion of these items in aggregate demand models is similarly problematic (as demonstrated by the baby food example presented in the introduction). While a simple point, the literature has failed to recognize this problem.

## 5    Monte Carlo Analysis

The previous section demonstrated that many products have limited retail distribution. We now explore the implications of this finding, specifically whether aggregate demand models that ignore product availability give biased estimates. Due to the difficulty of analytically determining the bias from estimating a mis-specified model, we rely upon Monte Carlo analysis.

The data used in the Monte Carlo simulations is generated assuming demand is determined by a standard logit framework. This specification is chosen for two reasons. First, it requires a small number of demand parameters. This is a key consideration when estimating demand for a large set of products since other commonly employed specifications, such as the constant elasticity or AIDS demand models, become unviable when the number of estimation parameters becomes too large.

A second feature of the logit demand model is that it can be quickly estimated. That is important since it is impractical to estimate a computationally burdensome model for a large number of Monte Carlo simulations. This requirement excludes the widely employed random coefficients logit demand specification (Nevo 2000). The popularity of that framework derives from its ability to accommodate more flexible substitution patterns than the standard logit model, where consumer substitution is proportional to market share. While the inflexibility of the standard logit model is a concern in empirical applications where proportional substitution may be violated, it is not a problem here since we generate the data employed in the Monte Carlo simulations assuming it is the correct framework.[7]

The following details the demand specification employed. There exist markets $m=1,2,\ldots,M$, where each represents a particular retailer-city for a given week. Consumer $i$ in market $m$ visits a single store and chooses either from among the products available at that store or chooses the "outside good." We normalize the utility from purchasing the outside good to a mean value of zero, $U_{i0m} = \omega_{i0m}$, where $\omega_{i0m}$ is i.i.d. Type I Extreme Value. For the remaining items, the utility derived from purchasing product $j$ is a function of observed characteristics $X_{jm}$, unobserved characteristics $\varepsilon_{jm}$ distributed i.i.d. $N(0,\sigma^2)$, and an idiosyncratic stochastic term $\omega_{ijm}$ that is i.i.d. Type I Extreme Value.

(5.1)  $U_{ijm} = X_{jm}\beta + \varepsilon_{jm} + \omega_{ijm}$

The set of observed characteristics $X_{jm}$ includes price and a retailer-city specific product fixed effect. We assume these characteristics do not vary across the stores in a given

---

[7] The problem of ignoring limited product availability when estimating aggregate demand is not specific to the logit framework. In a companion paper (Tenn 2006a), we show that very similar results can be obtained for the linear demand model (which, unlike the logit, accommodates flexible substitution patterns). Namely, cross-price elasticities are biased towards zero in the linear demand model when limited retail distribution is ignored. The extent of the bias depends on the probability a store carries one product conditional on it carrying the other.

market. This precludes the possibility that each store charges a different price. Researchers routinely invoke this assumption when estimating demand using aggregate data (e.g., Nevo 2001, Hausman and Leonard 2002). They do so because aggregate datasets do not report store-level prices. We similarly maintain this assumption since its possible violation is tangential to our analysis of whether ignoring limited product availability leads to biased estimates.[8]

Each market is composed of stores $s=1,2,...,S$, with each consumer randomly choosing to shop at a particular store. Stores vary solely with respect to the set of products, $J_{ms} \subseteq J_m$, that each carries. Let $A_{jms}$ denote an indicator variable for whether product $j$ is available in store $s$ in market $m$. The functional form assumptions provided above imply that product $j$'s market share $\pi_{jm}$ is as follows.

$$(5.2) \quad \pi_{jm} = \frac{1}{S}\sum_s \pi_{jms}, \text{ where } \pi_{jms} = \frac{A_{jms}e^{X_{jm}\beta + \varepsilon_{jm}}}{1 + \sum_{k \in J_m} A_{kms}e^{X_{km}\beta + \varepsilon_{km}}}$$

It is straightforward to derive the following formulas for each product's own- and cross-price elasticity at a particular store, where $\beta_p$ denotes the price coefficient from consumer utility function (5.1) and $p_{jm}$ is product $j$'s price in market $m$.

$$(5.3) \quad e_{jjms} = -\beta_p p_{jm}(1 - \pi_{jms}), \quad \forall j \in J_{ms}$$
$$e_{kjms} = \beta_p p_{jm}\pi_{jms}, \quad \forall j,k \in J_{ms} : j \neq k$$

Researchers typically report the average cross-price elasticity between two products for the set of consumers who have both items in their choice set (e.g., Berry et al. 1995, Nevo 2001).[9] Researchers do not report the average elasticity across *all* consumers, since doing so would underestimate the degree consumers view two products as substitutes. We follow

---

[8] Of course, conditional on there being one model mis-specification, a second mis-specification can either amplify or attenuate the bias.

[9] Note, however, while we assume consumers choose only between those products available at a particular store, the cited authors assume each consumer's choice set includes any product available in at least one store in a given market.

standard practice and calculate the average elasticity across the subset of consumers for which a given pair of items is in their choice set.

(5.4)  $e_{kj} = E_{ms}(e_{kjms} \mid A_{kms} = 1, A_{jms} = 1)$

This "heterogeneous store logit" framework is assumed to be the true model in the Monte Carlo analysis. We compare this framework to a "representative store logit" model that is otherwise identical, but assumes all stores carry the entire set of available products $J_m$. In that specification product $j$'s market share is as follows.

(5.5)  $\tilde{\pi}_{jm} = \dfrac{e^{X_{jm}\beta + \varepsilon_{jm}}}{1 + \sum\limits_{k \in J_m} e^{X_{km}\beta + \varepsilon_{km}}}$

Store- and aggregate-level elasticities take the following form in the standard logit model.

(5.6)  $\tilde{e}_{jjm} = -\beta_p P_{jm}(1 - \tilde{\pi}_{jm}),$   $\forall j \in J_m$

$\tilde{e}_{kjm} = \beta_p P_{jm}\tilde{\pi}_{jm},$   $\forall j, k \in J_m : j \neq k$

(5.7)  $\tilde{e}_{kj} = E_m(\tilde{e}_{kjm} \mid j, k \in J_m)$

A comparison of the elasticity formulas for the two models suggests three reasons one might obtain biased results if the representative store model is employed when the heterogeneous store framework is the correct specification. First, while the heterogeneous store logit recognizes that only a subset of stores in a market may carry a given pair of products, the representative store model assumes that either all or no stores in a given market carry both items. This can lead to the type of situation described in the introduction regarding baby food. It could be the case that no store carries both Heinz and Beech-Nut. If so, the cross-price elasticity between the two would not be defined in the heterogeneous store logit model. In contrast, the representative store logit would still produce an estimate for this (non-existent) cross-price elasticity.

A second difference pertains to how a product's market share is calculated. In the heterogeneous store logit model elasticities depend on a product's market share in those stores where it is available. In contrast, elasticities in the representative store model depend on a product's average market share across all stores. These two measures coincide when all stores are identical. When that assumption is violated, however, market shares in the two models can substantially diverge.

The last potential difference between the two models relates to price coefficient $\beta_p$. If the true model is the heterogeneous store logit, but one instead employs the representative store logit framework, one might expect to obtain a biased estimate for this parameter (although the direction and magnitude of the bias is hard to predict).

It is difficult to determine analytically the net impact of these factors. To provide some intuition for the Monte Carlo results presented below we consider a special case. Suppose product $j$ is available only in market $m$, and this product is carried by a fraction $ACV_{jm}$ of stores in that market. In addition, assume that product $j$'s market share is identical across all stores where it is available. Let $e_{jj}^{bias} = \tilde{e}_{jj} / e_{jj} - 1$ denote the percent bias of the own-price elasticity estimate from the representative store model when the heterogeneous store logit is the correct framework (where $e_{jj}$ and $\tilde{e}_{jj}$ are defined in equations (5.4) and (5.7), respectively). This term simplifies as follows in our simple example, where $\beta_p^{bias}$ denotes the percent bias in the price coefficient.

$$(5.8) \quad e_{jj}^{bias} = (1 + \beta_p^{bias}) \frac{1 - \pi_{jm}}{1 - \dfrac{\pi_{jm}}{ACV_{jm}}} - 1$$

Bias in the own-price elasticity is the product of two factors. The first is the percent bias in price coefficient $\beta_p$, which can be in either direction. The second term, $\dfrac{1 - \pi_{jm}}{1 - \dfrac{\pi_{jm}}{ACV_{jm}}}$, depends on a product's market share in those stores where it is available as well as its market share across all stores. This term causes the own-price elasticity to be (weakly) upwards biased (too elastic). Since $\beta_p^{bias}$ can be positive or negative, however, it is impossible to sign the overall bias. Consider the case where each product has a small market share in those stores where it is available. The term $\dfrac{1 - \pi_{jm}}{1 - \dfrac{\pi_{jm}}{ACV_{jm}}}$ limits to a value of one as a product's market share

grows increasingly small, so that the own-price elasticity bias approximately equals $\beta_p^{bias}$.

While it is not possible to predict the direction of bias, one would expect each product's own-price elasticity to be similarly biased since $\beta_p$ is not a product-specific parameter. This special case is empirically relevant when estimating the demand for a large number of products, where often no single product has a large market share. In our data, $\dfrac{1 - \pi_{jm}}{1 - \dfrac{\pi_{jm}}{ACV_{jm}}}$ has a value extremely

close to one for most products and is never larger than 1.03.[10] As such, in our Monte Carlo results one would expect the bias in each product's own-price elasticity to approximately equal $\beta_p^{bias}$. As discussed below, this is what we find.

We now consider the bias in the cross-price elasticity estimate from the representative store model when the heterogeneous store logit is the correct framework. Let $e_{kj}^{bias} = \tilde{e}_{kj} / e_{kj} - 1$ denote the percent bias in the cross-price elasticity. This term depends on $ACV_{kjm}$, the fraction of stores in market $m$ that carry both products $k$ and $j$. In our simple example, $e_{kj}^{bias}$ simplifies as follows.

$$(5.9) \quad e_{kj}^{bias} = (1 + \beta_p^{bias}) \frac{ACV_{kjm}}{ACV_{km}} - 1, \ \forall k \in J_m : j \neq k$$

As before, bias in price coefficient $\beta_p$ can be in either direction. The second factor, $\dfrac{ACV_{kjm}}{ACV_{km}}$, is the probability that product $j$ is available conditional on product $k$ being available.

This term causes the cross-price elasticity to be (weakly) downwards biased. In the Monte Carlo results, for most products this latter term dominates. The cross-price elasticity estimates are

---

[10] To calculate market shares researchers typically make an assumption regarding per-capita consumption, and then calculate a market's size using population data. Since we do not know the number of people who visit each retail chain, we follow Tenn (2006b) and instead assume each retailer-city's market size is ten times average category sales.

therefore biased towards zero on average, albeit with significant variation depending on the extent of a product's availability.[11]

We now turn to the Monte Carlo analysis, which allows us to consider situations where the bias from ignoring limited distribution cannot be analytically determined. To calibrate the model, we use the scanner data described in section 3 to estimate the heterogeneous store logit framework and obtain estimates for model parameters $\beta$ and $\sigma$. When doing so we restrict the data to products with either intermediate or wide distribution (i.e., products with median availability of at least 50% of stores). Although many products have low availability, they account for a very small fraction of dollar sales (see Table 1). As discussed earlier, the limited retail availability of such products is less of a concern since researchers often exclude low-selling items when estimating demand. To be conservative we follow this practice and remove such products. If we were to include them, however, our results would show an even larger bias from ignoring limited product availability.

Calibration of the heterogeneous store model requires three steps. First, we choose which stores in a market carry a given set of products. We assume each market is composed of 100 stores, and then randomly assign which products are available in a particular store.[12] For example, if a product is available in 50% of stores, we randomly select which 50 stores carry that item. Following Berry (1994), we then define $\delta_{jm} = X_{jm}\beta + \varepsilon_{jm}$ and iteratively solve for the set $\{\delta_{jm}\}_{\forall j,m}$ so that predicted market shares exactly equal observed market shares. Lastly, we estimate the linear equation $\delta_{jm} = X_{jm}\beta + \varepsilon_{jm}$ by ordinary least squares to obtain estimates of model parameters $\beta$ and $\sigma$.

---

[11] As detailed below, in the Monte Carlo analysis we assume each product's retail availability is independently distributed. Equation (5.9) simplifies to $e_{kj}^{bias} = (1 + \beta_p^{bias})ACV_{jm} - 1$ when $ACV_{kjm} = ACV_{km}ACV_{jm}$.

[12] As discussed later in the section, alternative assumptions for the joint distribution of product availability can lead to either smaller or larger bias.

These estimates are taken as the "true" parameter values from which we construct simulated data for each Monte Carlo simulation. We recognize that the obtained demand estimates might be biased for a variety of reasons, such as endogeneity bias, omitted variables bias, and the use of a restrictive functional form. Nonetheless, it allows us to calibrate the model in a way that approximates a real-world setting, and from which we can conduct a Monte Carlo analysis that by construction does not suffer from any of these potential biases.[13]

We conduct 2,500 Monte Carlo simulations, each of which is carried out as follows. Using the parameter estimates and control variables (but not the unit sales data) from the heterogeneous store logit model, we simulate a new dataset. We then use the simulated data to estimate the representative store logit model. The Berry inversion method is again relied upon to estimate the model via ordinary least squares, although $\{\delta_{jm}\}_{\forall j,m}$ is now calculated analytically. By comparing the estimated results to the true parameter values, we analyze whether ignoring limited retail distribution leads to biased findings.

The first panel of Table 2 reports the parameter estimates used to calibrate the heterogeneous store logit model. The average own-price elasticity ranges from -1.97 to -2.22, depending on the category. Cross-price elasticities are generally very small across all five product categories. The reason is that most products have relatively small market shares. Such products tend not to be close substitutes, since substitution is proportional to market share in the logit demand model.

The second panel in Table 2 reports the percent bias of the estimates produced by the representative store logit framework when the heterogeneous store logit is the correct model. Bias is estimated as the percent difference between the true value and the average estimate across the 2,500 Monte Carlo simulations.[14] Note that due to the large number of products in each

---

[13] Alternatively, we could have simply picked parameter values in a completely arbitrary manner.

[14] Since we employ a large number of simulations, variation due to random sampling has a negligible impact on the reported results.

category, it is not possible to report the percent bias for each individual own- and cross-price elasticity. Instead, we report the average percent bias across all products in each category. In addition, we report the standard deviation of the percent bias to measure the extent the bias varies across products.

The average own-price elasticity bias ranges from 4.2% to 18.3%, depending on the category. There is very little heterogeneity in the percent bias across products, with the standard deviation ranging from 1.3% to 2.2%. The special case considered earlier provides the intuition for why this occurs. Since most products have relatively small market shares, the percent bias approximately equals $\beta_p^{bias}$ for most items.

The average cross-price elasticity bias is somewhat larger, ranging from -10.6% to -20.7% depending on the category. Moreover, there is substantially more variation in the degree of bias across products. The standard deviation in the percent bias ranges from 16.1% to 19.7%. Again, the special case considered earlier suggests why this occurs. Recall that the cross-price elasticity bias largely depends on the extent of a product's availability. Since the median retail distribution of the products in the data sample ranges from 50% to 100% of stores, one would also expect the percent bias in the estimates to vary widely across products.

To provide a better indication of this, Figure 1 presents a histogram of the cross-price elasticity percent bias in the hot dog category. While the percent bias is positive for a few items, the cross-price elasticity is biased towards zero for most products. The degree of bias widely varies, however. While a percent bias close to zero most frequently occurs, percent biases as large as -50% are relatively common. We selected this category since the percent bias is not particularly big or small; histograms for the other product categories reveal a similar pattern.

The poor performance of the representative store model raises the issue of whether one might instead estimate demand using a framework that explicitly accounts for product assortment heterogeneity across stores, such as the heterogeneous store logit model employed above (or, more likely, a random coefficients variant that accommodates flexible substitution patterns). The problem with doing so is that the heterogeneous store model has informational requirements that go beyond what is reported in aggregate datasets. Specifically, evaluation of equation (5.2) requires the joint distribution of retail availability across all products (i.e., the fraction of stores that carry only a particular subset of items). Aggregate datasets typically used in demand estimation, such as scanner data produced by ACNielsen and IRI, do not report this joint distribution. They report only the univariate distribution of product availability (i.e., the fraction of stores that carry a particular item). We deal with this data deficiency in the Monte Carlo analysis by assuming each product's retail availability is independently distributed, so that the (observed) univariate distribution is sufficient to construct the (unobserved) joint distribution. While an interesting baseline case to consider, this independence assumption may be violated in empirical applications.

It is impossible to model heterogeneity in consumer choice sets without knowing the joint distribution of product availability. A continuum of joint distributions can potentially arise given a set of observed univariate distributions. Aggregate datasets do not report any information that identifies which of the many possible joint distributions is correct. Obviously, one cannot control for heterogeneity in product assortment across stores if the fraction of stores that carry a given set of items is not known.

One solution to this problem is to obtain better data. While ACNielsen and IRI do not report the joint distribution of product availability in the aggregate datasets they produce, this information is reported in their store-level datasets. Unfortunately, such data is far more expensive, and these vendors are often unwilling to provide data for a large number of stores (Boatwright et al. 2004). The widespread use of aggregate data to estimate demand likely indicates many researchers lack access to store-level data.

When store-level data is unavailable, an alternative approach is to estimate the heterogeneous store model under a wide range of assumptions for the joint distribution of retail availability. One would have greater confidence in those estimates that are insensitive to the joint distribution assumed. Conversely, the data contains insufficient information to identify the estimates that significantly vary depending on the joint distribution employed.

An alternative approach is to rely upon a representative store model, but then undertake sensitivity analysis regarding the likely bias from doing so. Consider the example discussed earlier for which equation (5.9) reports $e_{kj}^{bias}$, the percent bias of the cross-price elasticity estimate from the representative store logit model when the heterogeneous store logit is the correct framework. The degree of bias crucially depends on $ACV_{kjm}$, the fraction of stores in market $m$ that carry both products $k$ and $j$. As discussed above, $ACV_{kjm}$ is not reported in aggregate datasets. Nonetheless, one can place bounds on the range of values $ACV_{kjm}$ can take. The smallest possible value for this term is $ACV_{kjm}^{min} = \max(0, ACV_{km} + ACV_{jm} - 1)$, while the largest possible value is $ACV_{kjm}^{max} = \min(ACV_{km}, ACV_{jm})$.

When $[ACV_{kjm}^{min}, ACV_{kjm}^{max}]$ contains a narrow range of values, one has a good sense of the likely bias from using the representative store model. For example, suppose products $k$ and $j$ are each available in 50% of stores. Further, assume the percent bias in the estimated price coefficient is sufficiently small that it can be ignored (i.e., $\beta_p^{bias} \approx 0$). In this case, equation (5.9) implies $e_{kj}^{bias} \in [-100\%, 0\%]$. The estimated cross-price elasticity might be unbiased, or it could be underestimated by 100%. Since we do not know the true magnitude of the bias, the estimated cross-price elasticity has little informative value. In contrast, suppose products $k$ and $j$ are each available in 95% of stores. Equation (5.9) implies $e_{kj}^{bias} \in [-10\%, 0\%]$. Since $e_{kj}^{bias}$ lies in a fairly narrow range, one would have a much better idea of the bias in the estimated cross-price elasticity for this latter example.

To summarize, aggregate data lacks the requisite information to explicitly model heterogeneous product availability across stores. In some situations, this is a fatal shortcoming since the estimated elasticities crucially depend on the unobserved joint distribution of retail availability. In other cases, this joint distribution plays less of a role. Researchers can undertake the sensitivity analyses suggested above to determine whether an aggregate demand model might be successfully employed in a particular situation.

## 6  Explanations for Limited Distribution

In this section, we explore why so many products have limited retail distribution. We do so for two reasons. First, a better understanding of the empirical determinants of product availability would clearly be useful given that retail distribution touches on a number of distinct literatures as mentioned in section 2. The second reason is directly applicable to the focus of this paper; by obtaining a better understanding of why products have limited distribution, researchers may be more attuned to whether limited product availability is likely to be a significant problem in a particular demand application.

As discussed earlier, products with low retail distribution pose only a minor problem when estimating demand. Such products account for a small percentage of sales, and therefore can be reasonably omitted from the analysis altogether. For that reason, in this section we focus on products with intermediate distribution. Also, note that new and discontinued items are excluded from the analysis, except for when we explicitly consider them. Doing so allows us to differentiate between reasons why products have limited retail distribution on a transitional basis, as opposed to consistently having limited distribution.

Product-Line Length

One explanation for why products have limited availability is that it is impractical for retailers to carry entire product lines due to space limitations and consumer preference heterogeneity across stores.[15] Rather, they typically carry only a subset of the UPCs contained within each line of products (e.g., Lemon-Lime Gatorade but not Lemonade Gatorade). We explore whether heterogeneity in product assortment explains why so many items are available in most, but not all of a retailer's stores. If products with limited distribution are secondary

---

[15] Retailers often optimize the product assortment at a particular store to account for heterogeneity in consumer preferences. Since this issue is addressed in previous research, such as Stassen et al. (1999), we do not focus on that explanation here.

package sizes or varieties of widely available products, that could explain why many stores do not carry such items.

The dataset includes three types of product characteristics that describe each UPC. The first defines the set of UPCs that constitutes a given product line. For example, "Ben & Jerry's ice cream" and "Ben & Jerry's frozen yogurt" are distinct product lines. The other characteristics describe each product's package size and variety. In the ice cream category, for example, variety is measured by characteristics such as flavor (e.g., vanilla), fat-content (e.g., "low-fat"), and sugar-content (e.g., "no sugar added"). Each UPC within a product line is defined by a unique combination of package size and variety characteristics.

We use these characteristics to compute statistics regarding whether the other members of a UPC's product line are widely available. As indicated earlier, we employ a data sample composed of products with intermediate distribution (i.e., products with median availability of 50% to 90% of stores). The first row of Table 3 reports the fraction of UPCs that are part of widely available product lines. This is defined as product lines where at least 90% of stores carry a UPC from that line (although each store may carry a different assortment of UPCs). A large percentage of UPCs with intermediate distribution, 64% to 93% depending on the category, are part of widely available product lines. The second row of Table 3 shows that depending on the category, 22% to 66% of UPCs with intermediate distribution are from product lines where at least one UPC is widely available. The large difference between the first two rows of statistics demonstrates that even though stores largely carry the same product lines, they carry a different subset of items. Heterogeneity in product assortment is so extensive that it is often the case that no single UPC from a widely available product line is itself widely available.

The third and fourth rows of Table 3 examine whether product assortment heterogeneity is due to differences in product variety or package size. We find that only a small fraction of items are alternative package sizes of widely available product varieties. Depending on the category, this is the case for only 1% to 12% of UPCs. In contrast, 20% to 64% of UPCs are from product lines that contain a widely available item with the same package size, but a different variety. Thus, product assortment differences are primarily due to certain stores not carrying all of the varieties contained within a product line, rather than from stores not carrying secondary package sizes.

New Product Introductions

Another reason many products have limited retail distribution is that the process of introducing and discontinuing items often takes place over many weeks. Even if a product eventually becomes widely available, during a transition period it is typically carried by only a subset of a retailer's stores. To show this, we look at how long it takes a new product to become widely available. One slight complication is that we have only 132 weeks of data, which leads to a truncation problem for products introduced towards the end of the dataset. To avoid truncation bias, we estimate a duration model and then calculate the probability of a given introduction spell length using the estimated model parameters.

We restrict the data sample to newly introduced products, and then estimate the following model. Let $A_{jrt}$ denote an indicator variable for whether product $j$ is available in at least one store in retailer-city $r$ in week $t$ (i.e., $ACV_{jrt} > 0$). Similarly, let $W_{jrt}$ denote an indicator variable for whether product $j$ is widely available (i.e., $ACV_{jrt} \geq 90\%$). We rely on a two equation discrete-time duration model where $A_{jrt}$ and $W_{jrt}$ are the dependent variables, respectively, $X_{jrt}$ is a set of observed product characteristics, and $\Lambda$ denotes the logistic cumulative distribution function.

$$(6.1) \quad P(A_{jrt} = 1 \mid A_{jr,t-1} = 1) = \Lambda(X_{jrt}\beta_1)$$
$$P(W_{jrt} = 1 \mid A_{jrt} = 1, W_{jr,t-1} = 0) = \Lambda(X_{jrt}\beta_2)$$

Becoming widely available ($W_{jrt} = 1$) and being discontinued ($A_{jrt} = 0$) are both terminal conditions that end the introduction spell. This spell continues for as long as a product remains available, but not widely available (or the dataset ends, in which case the introduction spell is truncated).

To accommodate either positive or negative duration dependence, the set of control variables $X_{jrt}$ includes a fourth order polynomial in the number of weeks since a product was introduced. In addition, it consists of a set of dummy variables for the calendar month, and a set of retailer-city dummy variables that control for heterogeneity with respect to how quickly retailers introduce or discontinue items. Lastly, we include the four variables shown in Table 3, which control for whether an item is from a widely available product line, whether that line includes a widely available item, and whether that line contains a widely available UPC of the same variety or package size. We construct these measures using data from the week prior to when an item is first introduced. They are included in the set of control variables since the availability of related products potentially speaks to whether a newly introduced item will itself become widely available.

The estimation results from the two logit models are presented in Table 4. It is difficult to tell from the parameter estimates what the fourth order polynomial in the number of weeks since a product was introduced looks like. Therefore, we briefly describe its profile, which is similar across the five product categories. In the first model where the dependent variable is $A_{jrt}$, the probability of being discontinued is highest for products that have just been introduced. It gradually decreases until approximately 20 weeks following the product introduction, after which the probability starts to increase again. Similarly, when $W_{jrt}$ is the dependent variable, the probability of becoming widely available in a given period peaks at around 10 weeks and then gradually declines. As shown in the table, mixed results are obtained for the remaining control variables that measure the availability of the other items in the same product line. In some categories a new product from a widely available product line is more likely to become widely available itself, while the opposite is true in other categories.

For each product $j$, the set of control variables $X_{jrt}$ and parameters $\beta_1$ and $\beta_2$ are used to predict the likelihood of a given spell outcome and duration. The first panel in Table 5 reports the probability of becoming either widely available or being discontinued in the first year, as well as the probability that the introduction spell has not been completed by the end of the first year (i.e., a product is available, but not widely available). While the results vary somewhat by product category, on average approximately one third of new products become widely available in the first year, and an additional one third are discontinued. That leaves the remaining one third of products, which continue to be available, but with limited distribution. Depending on the category, in its first year a new product has limited product availability an average of 21.4 to 36.1 weeks.

The second panel of Table 5 presents the probability of becoming widely available in a given week, conditional on a product becoming widely available in its first year. Many products quickly become widely available, with 18% to 43% of products doing so in their first month, depending on the category. Nonetheless, most products take substantial longer, with an average of 8.6 to 14.2 weeks. The third panel of Table 5 presents the probability of being discontinued in a particular week conditional on a product being discontinued in its first year. In general, it takes longer for a new product to be discontinued, with an average of 16.1 to 21.1 weeks depending on the category.

To summarize, product introductions are not an instantaneous process. To the contrary, new products undergo a lengthy transition where approximately two thirds are either discontinued or become widely available within a year. Since that transition often takes many weeks, a new product typically has limited retail distribution for much of its first year.

Other Sources of Intertemporal Variation

Even established products often experience temporary changes in distribution. One reason is that widely available UPCs occasionally have stock-outs. To demonstrate this, we restrict the data sample to widely available products. Table 6 shows that very few of these products are widely available *every* week. Depending on the category, 66% to 79% of UPCs are available in 50% to 90% of stores during at least one week. However, few of these products are ever available in less than 50% of stores. Depending on the category, this is the case for only 7% to 19% of UPCs.

While creating an exhaustive list of reasons for why retail distribution changes over time is beyond the scope of this paper, it is worth pointing out that nearly all products undergo extensive intertemporal variation in product availability. To show this we estimate the following model, separately for each product $j$.

$$(6.2) \quad \ln(ACV_{jrt}) = \delta_{jt} + \delta_{jr} + \alpha_{1jr}t + \alpha_{2jr}t^2 + \varepsilon_{jrt}, \text{ where } Var(\varepsilon_{jrt}) = \sigma_j^2.$$

Each product's log distribution (ACV) is regressed against a set of fixed effects for time $t$ and retailer-city $r$, and a retailer-city specific quadratic time trend. The root mean squared error (RMSE) from the regression, $\hat{\sigma}_j$, measures the extent distribution is changing over time after accounting for these factors. We include these controls to demonstrate that distributional changes are idiosyncratic, and are not implicitly controlled for in models that account for underlying trends or seasonality. Since time fixed effects and quadratic time trends are commonly used, that is the specification we chose to employ.

Table 7 presents the distribution of the RMSE estimates obtained from equation (6.2).[16] The results show substantial variation in product distribution over time, with a median RMSE of 9% to 16%, depending on the category. Most products have either intermediate variability (RMSE between 10% and 20%) or high variability (RMSE of 20% or more). Not only is limited product availability extremely common, but the extent of most products' retail distribution significantly varies over time.

## 7 Conclusion

Aggregate demand models typically assume all consumers in a given market shop at the same "representative store," and therefore face the same choice set. We find little empirical support for this assumption. Across the five grocery categories in our dataset, products with

---

[16] Equation (6.2) requires a sufficient number of observations to estimate the RMSE with reasonable precision. The approach taken here is to include all products with at least 156 weeks (three years) of observations (out of a maximum possible 1,848 pooled weeks). The results are not sensitive to this choice of sample selection.

limited retail distribution represent a large percentage of category sales. Thus, consumers in the same market have very different choice sets depending on where they shop.

Monte Carlo analysis shows that the observed level of limited retail distribution is sufficient to bias significantly own- and cross-price elasticity estimates in models that do not control for the extent of a product's retail distribution. While it is obvious that limited product availability can affect demand analysis in highly atypical conditions such as the baby food example discussed earlier, our results indicate the bias from ignoring limited retail distribution can be quite large even under ordinary conditions.

We find support for three hypotheses regarding why so many products have limited retail distribution: (1) stores carry select varieties of popular product lines, rather than the entire line; (2) new product introductions often take place over a period of months—not weeks; and (3) even top-selling, widely distributed products have occasional stock-outs that temporarily reduce their retail distribution. By providing a better understanding of why products have limited retail distribution, we hope researchers will be more attuned to whether this is likely to be an issue in a particular demand application.

Finally, while our results show that representative store aggregate demand models may perform quite poorly, researchers who lack store-level data have few alternatives since aggregate datasets contain insufficient information to control for product assortment heterogeneity across stores. Nonetheless, the sensitivity analyses we suggest allow researchers to assess the likely magnitude of the bias. This gives researchers some degree of certainty regarding whether an aggregate demand model might be successfully employed in a particular circumstance, or whether store-level data is ultimately required.

**References**

Asker, John, "Measuring Advantages from Exclusive Dealing," working paper, April 2004a.

Asker, John, "Diagnosing Foreclosure Due to Exclusive Dealing," working paper, October 2004b.

Bergen, Mark, Shantanu Dutta, and Steven M. Shugan, "Branded Variants: A Retail Perspective," *Journal of Marketing Research* 33 (1996), pp. 9-19.

Berry, Steven T., "Estimating Discrete-Choice Models of Product Differentiation," *RAND Journal of Economics* 25 (1994), pp. 242-262.

Berry, Steven, James Levinsohn, and Ariel Pakes, "Automobile Prices in Market Equilibrium," *Econometrica* 63 (1995), pp. 841-90.

Besanko, David, Jean-Pierre Dubé, and Sachin Gupta, "Competitive Price Discrimination Strategies in a Vertical Channel Using Aggregate Retail Data," *Management Science* 49 (2003), pp. 1121-38.

Boatwright, Peter, Sanjay Dhar, and Peter E. Rossi, "The Role of Retail Competition, Demographics and Account Retail Strategy as Drivers of Promotional Sensitivity," *Quantitative Marketing and Economics* 2 (2004), pp. 169-90.

Brenkers, Randy, and Frank Verboven, "Liberalizing a Distribution System: The European Car Market," working paper, November 2004.

Bronnenberg, Bart J., Vijay Mahajan, and Wilfried R. Vanhonacker, "The Emergence of Market Structure in New Repeat-Purchase Categories: The Interplay of Market Share and Retailer Distribution," *Journal of Marketing Research* 37 (2000), pp. 16-31.

Bucklin, Randolph E., and James M. Lattin, "A Model of Product Category Competition Among Grocery Retailers," *Journal of Retailing* 68 (1992), pp. 271-93.

Chintagunta, Pradeep K., "Investigating Category Pricing Behavior at a Retail Chain," *Journal of Marketing Research* 39 (2002), pp. 141-54.

Chintagunta, Pradeep K., Jean-Pierre Dubé, and Vishal Singh, "Balancing Profitability and Customer Welfare in a Supermarket Chain," *Quantitative Marketing and Economics* 1 (2003), pp. 111-47.

Cotterill, Ronald W., William P. Putsis, Jr., and Ravi Dhar, "Assessing the Competitive Interaction Between Private Labels and National Brands," *Journal of Business* 73 (2000), pp. 109-37.

Curhan, Ronald C., "The Relationship Between Shelf Space and Unit Sales in Supermarkets," *Journal of Marketing Research* 9 (1972), pp. 406-12.

Draganska, Michaela and Dipak Jain, "Product-Line Length as a Competitive Tool," *Journal of Economics and Management Strategy* 14 (2005), pp. 1-28.

Drèze, Xavier, Stephen J. Hoch, and Mary E. Purk, "Shelf Management and Space Elasticity," *Journal of Retailing* 70 (1994), pp. 301-26.

Farris, Paul, James Olver, and Cornelis De Kluyver, "The Relationship Between Distribution and Market Share," *Marketing Science* 2 (1989), pp. 107-28.

Gupta, Sachin, Pradeep Chintagunta, Anil Kaul, and Dick R. Wittink, "Do Household Scanner Data Provide Representative Inferences from Brand Choices: A Comparison with Store Level Data," *Journal of Marketing Research* 33 (1996), pp. 383-98.

Hausman, Jerry A. and Gregory K. Leonard, "The Competitive Effects of a New Product Introduction: A Case Study," *Journal of Industrial Economics* 50 (2002), pp. 237-63.

Hausman, Jerry, Gregory Leonard, and J. Douglas Zona, "Competitive Analysis with Differenciated Products," *Annales D'Économie et de Statistique* 34 (1994), pp. 159-80.

Heide, Jan B., Shantanu Dutta, and Mark Bergen, "Exclusive Dealing and Business Efficiency: Evidence From Industry Practice," *Journal of Law and Economics* 41 (1998), pp. 387-407.

Hoch, Stephen J., Byung-Do Kim, Alan L. Montgomery, and Peter E. Rossi, "Determinants of Store-Level Price Elasticity," *Journal of Marketing Research* 32 (1995), pp. 17-29.

Kumar, V. and Robert P. Leone, "Measuring the Effect of Retail Store and Promotions on Brand and Store Substitution," *Journal of Marketing Research* 25 (1988), pp. 178-85.

Lafontaine, Francine, "Agency Theory and Franchising: Some Empirical Results," *RAND Journal of Economics* 23 (1992), pp. 263-83.

Lafontaine, Francine and Kathryn L. Shaw, "The Dynamics of Franchise Contracting: Evidence from Pane Data," *Journal of Political Economy* 107 (1999), pp. 1041-80.

Lafontaine, Francine and Margaret Slade, "Retail Contracting: Theory and Practice," *Journal of Industrial Economics* 45 (1997), pp. 1-25.

Nevo, Aviv, "A Practitioner's Guide to Estimation of Random-Coefficients Logit Models of Demand," *Journal of Economics and Management Strategy* 9 (2000), pp., 513-548.

Nevo, Aviv, "Measuring Market Power in the Ready-to-Eat Cereal Industry," *Econometrica* 69 (2001), pp. 307-42.

Nevo, Aviv and Konstantinos Hatzitaskos, "Why Does the Average Price of Tuna Fall During Lent?," NBER Working Paper No. 11572, August 2005.

Olver, James M. and Paul W. Farris, "Push and Pull: A One-Two Punch for Packaged Products," *Sloan Management Review* 31 (1989), pp. 53-61.

Ornstein, Stanley I. and Dominique M. Hanssens, "Resale Price Maintenance: Output Increasing or Restricting? The Case of Distilled Spirits in the United States," *Journal of Industrial Economics* 36 (1987), pp. 1-18.

Pesendorfer, Martin, "Retail Sales: A Study of Pricing Behavior in Supermarkets," *Journal of Business* 75 (2002), pp. 33-66.

Petrin, Amil, "Quantifying the Benefits of New Products: The Case of the Minivan," *Journal of Political Economy* 110 (2002), pp. 705-29.

Reibstein, David J. and Paul W. Farris, "Market Share and Distribution: A Generalization, A Speculation, and Some Implications," *Marketing Science* 14 (1995), pp. 190-202.

Rhee, Hongjai and David R. Bell, "The Inter-Store Mobility of Supermarket Shoppers," *Journal of Retailing* 78 (2002), pp. 225-37.

Shaffer, Greg, "Slotting Allowances and Resale Price Maintenance: A Comparison of Facilitating Practices," *RAND Journal of Economics* 22 (1991), pp. 120-35.

Sullivan, Mary W., "Slotting Allowances and the Market for New Products," *Journal of Law and Economics* 40 (1997), pp. 461-93.

Stassen, Robert E., John D. Mittelstaedt, and Robert A. Mittelstaedt, "Assortment Overlap: Its Effect on Shopping Patterns in a Retail Market When the Distributions of Prices and Goods Are Known," *Journal of Retailing* 75 (1999), pp. 371-86.

Steiner, Robert L., "The Prejudice Against Marketing," *Journal of Marketing* 40 (1976), pp. 2-9.

Steiner, Robert L., "The Evolution and Applications of Dual-Stage Thinking," *Antitrust Bulletin* 49 (2004), pp. 877-909.

Tenn, Steven, "Demand Estimation under Limited Product Availability," working paper, August 2006a.

Tenn, Steven, "Avoiding Aggregation Bias in Demand Estimation: A Multivariate Promotional Disaggregation Approach," *Quantitative Marketing and Economics* 4 (2006b), pp. 383-405.

Villas-Boas, Sophia B., "Vertical Contracts Between Manufacturers and Retailers: Inference with Limited Data," CUDARE Working Paper 943R2, July 2005.

# Table 1

## Percent of Products, by Median Product Availability

| Available in % of Stores: | Frozen Novelty (N=3,123) | Pasta (N=5,127) | Hot Dog (N=1,176) | Ice Cream (N=6,345) | Salad Dressing (N=6,436) | Average |
|---|---|---|---|---|---|---|
| **Low Availability:** | | | | | | |
| 0% to 10% | 9% | 26% | 10% | 8% | 17% | 14% |
| 10% to 20% | 8% | 18% | 6% | 10% | 14% | 11% |
| 20% to 30% | 5% | 7% | 5% | 7% | 7% | 6% |
| 30% to 40% | 5% | 5% | 3% | 7% | 5% | 5% |
| 40% to 50% | 6% | 4% | 3% | 8% | 5% | 5% |
| Sub-total | 33% | 60% | 28% | 40% | 48% | 42% |
| **Intermediate Availability:** | | | | | | |
| 50% to 60% | 7% | 4% | 5% | 9% | 6% | 6% |
| 60% to 70% | 9% | 4% | 6% | 10% | 7% | 7% |
| 70% to 80% | 12% | 5% | 7% | 10% | 9% | 9% |
| 80% to 90% | 15% | 7% | 13% | 11% | 11% | 11% |
| Sub-total | 43% | 19% | 30% | 40% | 34% | 33% |
| **Wide Availability:** | | | | | | |
| 90% to 99% | 14% | 10% | 17% | 11% | 10% | 12% |
| 99% to 100% | 10% | 12% | 24% | 9% | 9% | 13% |
| Sub-total | 24% | 21% | 41% | 19% | 18% | 25% |

## Percent of Dollar Sales, by Median Product Availability

| Available in % of Stores: | Frozen Novelty | Pasta | Hot Dog | Ice Cream | Salad Dressing | Average |
|---|---|---|---|---|---|---|
| **Low Availability:** | | | | | | |
| 0% to 10% | 0% | 1% | 0% | 0% | 0% | 0% |
| 10% to 20% | 0% | 2% | 0% | 1% | 1% | 1% |
| 20% to 30% | 0% | 2% | 1% | 1% | 1% | 1% |
| 30% to 40% | 1% | 2% | 1% | 1% | 1% | 1% |
| 40% to 50% | 2% | 2% | 1% | 3% | 1% | 2% |
| Sub-total | 4% | 8% | 3% | 6% | 4% | 5% |
| **Intermediate Availability:** | | | | | | |
| 50% to 60% | 2% | 2% | 1% | 4% | 2% | 2% |
| 60% to 70% | 5% | 2% | 2% | 6% | 3% | 4% |
| 70% to 80% | 9% | 4% | 4% | 8% | 6% | 6% |
| 80% to 90% | 17% | 9% | 8% | 14% | 12% | 12% |
| Sub-total | 33% | 17% | 16% | 33% | 23% | 24% |
| **Wide Availability:** | | | | | | |
| 90% to 99% | 32% | 24% | 25% | 25% | 22% | 26% |
| 99% to 100% | 30% | 51% | 56% | 37% | 51% | 45% |
| Sub-total | 63% | 75% | 81% | 62% | 73% | 71% |

*Notes*: N = number of products, which is defined as a UPC in a given retailer-city. Each column sums to 100%.

## Table 2
## Monte Carlo Results

### A. Heterogeneous Store Logit Calibration

| | Frozen Novelty | | Pasta | | Hot Dog | | Ice Cream | | Salad Dressing | |
|---|---|---|---|---|---|---|---|---|---|---|
| | Est | | Est | | Est | | Est | | Est | |
| Price Coefficient | -0.75 | | -1.70 | | -0.75 | | -0.62 | | -0.85 | |
| $\sigma$ | 0.44 | | 0.39 | | 0.45 | | 0.40 | | 0.36 | |
| # of Observations | 200,004 | | 239,575 | | 86,573 | | 372,466 | | 341,544 | |
| | Avg | Std Dev | Avg | Std Dev | Avg | Std Dev | Avg | Std Dev | Avg | Std Dev |
| Own-Price Elasticity | -2.22 | 0.62 | -2.11 | 0.92 | -2.16 | 1.28 | -2.13 | 0.60 | -1.97 | 0.78 |
| Cross-Price Elasticity | 0.002 | 0.001 | 0.001 | 0.001 | 0.003 | 0.003 | 0.001 | 0.001 | 0.001 | 0.002 |

### B. Percent Bias of the Representative Store Logit when the Hetergeneous Store Logit is the Correct Model

| | Frozen Novelty | | Pasta | | Hot Dog | | Ice Cream | | Salad Dressing | |
|---|---|---|---|---|---|---|---|---|---|---|
| | Est | | Est | | Est | | Est | | Est | |
| Price Coefficient | 3.8% | | 6.3% | | 7.4% | | 16.8% | | 15.8% | |
| $\sigma$ | 30.0% | | 20.4% | | 13.5% | | 29.0% | | 33.9% | |
| | Avg | Std Dev | Avg | Std Dev | Avg | Std Dev | Avg | Std Dev | Avg | Std Dev |
| Own-Price Elasticity | 4.2% | 1.3% | 6.8% | 1.3% | 8.2% | 1.3% | 18.3% | 2.2% | 16.8% | 1.8% |
| Cross-Price Elasticity | -20.7% | 17.9% | -13.5% | 17.4% | -10.6% | 16.1% | -11.9% | 19.7% | -11.5% | 18.5% |

*Notes*: Panel A reports the parameter values used to simulate the data employed in the Monte Carlo analysis. Each observation in the demand analysis corresponds to a particular UPC in a given retailer-city in a given week. Panel B reports the average percent difference between the true and estimated values across the 2,500 Monte Carlo simulations.

28

## Table 3

### Percent of Intermediate Available Products, by Product Line Availability

| | Frozen Novelty (N=559) | Pasta (N=579) | Hot Dog (N=139) | Ice Cream (N=1,037) | Salad Dressing (N=948) | Average |
|---|---|---|---|---|---|---|
| Product Line is Widely Available | 80% | 81% | 64% | 93% | 86% | 81% |
| Product Line Contains a Widely Available UPC | 22% | 50% | 44% | 66% | 61% | 49% |
| Product Line Contains a Widely Available UPC of the Same Variety | 1% | 8% | 5% | 5% | 12% | 6% |
| Product Line Contains a Widely Available UPC with the Same Package Size | 20% | 39% | 27% | 64% | 49% | 40% |

*Notes:* N = number of products, which is defined as a UPC in a given retailer-city. The data sample is restricted to products with intermediate availability, which is defined as median retail distribution of 50% to 90% of stores. Widely available is defined as median retail distribution of 90% to 100% of stores.

## Table 4

## Logit Estimates, Product Introduction Duration Model

### A. Dependent Variable: Product is Available

| | Frozen Novelty | | Pasta | | Hot Dog | | Ice Cream | | Salad Dressing | |
|---|---|---|---|---|---|---|---|---|---|---|
| | Est | SE | Est | SE | Est | SE | Est | SE | Est | SE |
| Intercept | 4.36 | (0.39) *** | 3.51 | (0.23) *** | 3.13 | (0.54) *** | 4.06 | (0.30) *** | 4.31 | (0.22) *** |
| Time Elapsed | 22.25 | (3.92) *** | 20.48 | (2.52) *** | 22.53 | (6.20) *** | 27.52 | (3.17) *** | 18.06 | (2.20) *** |
| Time Elapsed^2 | -103.23 | (17.61) *** | -73.04 | (11.06) *** | -88.44 | (31.56) *** | -124.52 | (14.07) *** | -83.15 | (9.95) *** |
| Time Elapsed^3 | 159.96 | (28.77) *** | 99.69 | (17.52) *** | 128.00 | (57.45) ** | 190.60 | (22.44) *** | 133.64 | (16.19) *** |
| Time Elapsed^4 | -81.96 | (15.53) *** | -48.42 | (9.07) *** | -63.19 | (33.54) * | -96.52 | (11.80) *** | -71.55 | (8.63) *** |
| Product Line is Widely Available | -0.15 | (0.25) | 0.61 | (0.17) *** | -1.64 | (0.64) ** | 0.19 | (0.13) | 0.72 | (0.18) *** |
| Product Line Contains a Widely Available UPC | 0.17 | (0.28) | -0.05 | (0.28) | 2.04 | (0.72) *** | -0.30 | (0.19) | -0.40 | (0.21) * |
| Product Line Contains a Widely Available UPC of the Same Variety | -0.14 | (0.33) | -0.81 | (0.32) ** | -0.26 | (0.73) | 0.30 | (0.62) | -0.20 | (0.20) |
| Product Line Contains a Widely Available UPC with the Same Package Size | 0.21 | (0.22) | -0.43 | (0.27) | -0.47 | (0.45) | 0.30 | (0.16) * | -0.33 | (0.15) ** |
| # of Observations | 36,454 | | 82,987 | | 9,067 | | 77,732 | | 91,323 | |

### B. Dependent Variable: Product is Widely Available

| | Frozen Novelty | | Pasta | | Hot Dog | | Ice Cream | | Salad Dressing | |
|---|---|---|---|---|---|---|---|---|---|---|
| | Est | SE | Est | SE | Est | SE | Est | SE | Est | SE |
| Intercept | -7.60 | (0.50) *** | -7.20 | (0.39) *** | -6.37 | (0.74) *** | -5.19 | (0.24) *** | -7.17 | (0.27) *** |
| Time Elapsed | 15.55 | (3.58) *** | 18.02 | (5.15) *** | -5.09 | (5.08) | 20.14 | (2.57) *** | 18.53 | (2.86) *** |
| Time Elapsed^2 | -141.76 | (26.69) *** | -129.76 | (35.50) *** | -53.81 | (37.75) | -183.36 | (19.45) *** | -147.17 | (20.62) *** |
| Time Elapsed^3 | 305.25 | (63.45) *** | 228.88 | (78.58) *** | 180.19 | (89.22) ** | 381.47 | (45.75) *** | 284.38 | (47.17) *** |
| Time Elapsed^4 | -194.25 | (46.21) *** | -121.57 | (53.77) ** | -140.62 | (64.84) ** | -233.69 | (33.23) *** | -165.34 | (33.22) *** |
| Product Line is Widely Available | -0.33 | (0.21) | 0.60 | (0.35) * | 0.39 | (0.70) | -0.53 | (0.12) *** | 0.92 | (0.15) *** |
| Product Line Contains a Widely Available UPC | 0.23 | (0.23) | 1.76 | (0.36) *** | 0.21 | (0.70) | 0.63 | (0.14) *** | 0.39 | (0.15) ** |
| Product Line Contains a Widely Available UPC of the Same Variety | -0.73 | (0.31) ** | 0.25 | (0.27) | 0.29 | (0.42) | -0.01 | (0.27) | 0.48 | (0.12) *** |
| Product Line Contains a Widely Available UPC with the Same Package Size | -0.09 | (0.16) | 0.76 | (0.18) *** | 0.27 | (0.24) | -0.18 | (0.10) * | 0.39 | (0.10) *** |
| # of Observations | 37,462 | | 83,851 | | 9,318 | | 79,667 | | 92,964 | |

*Notes*: The data sample is restricted to new products. Each observation corresponds to a particular UPC in a given retailer-city in a given week. Both models also include a set of dummy variables for the calendar month and a set of retailer-city fixed effects. Robust standard errors that are clustered by product are reported. Significance levels correspond to *=10%, **=5%, ***=1%. For clearer presentation, "time elapsed" is rescaled by dividing by 132 weeks, so that this variable takes values between 0 and 1.

## Table 5

## Spell Length Predicted Probabilities for New Product Introductions

### A. Outcome in First Year Following Product Introduction

| | Frozen Novelty (N=1,340) | Pasta (N=1,631) | Hot Dog (N=358) | Ice Cream (N=2,581) | Salad Dressing (N=2,634) | Average |
|---|---|---|---|---|---|---|
| | % of Products | | | | | |
| % Widely Available | 17% | 27% | 49% | 51% | 26% | 34% |
| % Available, But Not Widely Available | 34% | 57% | 27% | 34% | 41% | 39% |
| % Discontinued | 49% | 17% | 24% | 15% | 33% | 28% |
| Total | 100% | 100% | 100% | 100% | 100% | 100% |
| | Weeks in First Year with Limited Distribution | | | | | |
| Average weeks | 25.3 | 36.1 | 21.4 | 25.5 | 30.6 | 27.8 |
| Median weeks | 15.0 | 52.0 | 10.0 | 16.0 | 33.0 | 25.2 |

### B. Duration, Conditional on Becoming Widely Available in First Year

| | Frozen Novelty | Pasta | Hot Dog | Ice Cream | Salad Dressing | Average |
|---|---|---|---|---|---|---|
| | % of Products | | | | | |
| 1-4 weeks | 29% | 18% | 43% | 26% | 19% | 27% |
| 5-8 weeks | 26% | 20% | 23% | 26% | 21% | 23% |
| 9-12 weeks | 19% | 16% | 13% | 18% | 19% | 17% |
| 13-26 weeks | 20% | 33% | 15% | 24% | 32% | 25% |
| 27-39 weeks | 4% | 10% | 4% | 4% | 7% | 6% |
| 40-52 weeks | 2% | 3% | 2% | 1% | 2% | 2% |
| Total | 100% | 100% | 100% | 100% | 100% | 100% |
| Average weeks | 10.1 | 14.2 | 8.6 | 10.3 | 12.8 | 11.2 |
| Median weeks | 8.0 | 11.0 | 5.0 | 8.0 | 10.0 | 8.4 |

### C. Duration, Conditional on Being Discontinued in First Year

| | Frozen Novelty | Pasta | Hot Dog | Ice Cream | Salad Dressing | Average |
|---|---|---|---|---|---|---|
| | % of Products | | | | | |
| 1-4 weeks | 20% | 21% | 28% | 25% | 17% | 22% |
| 5-8 weeks | 16% | 18% | 19% | 16% | 15% | 17% |
| 9-12 weeks | 11% | 12% | 11% | 9% | 10% | 11% |
| 13-26 weeks | 19% | 23% | 18% | 14% | 22% | 19% |
| 27-39 weeks | 13% | 13% | 11% | 11% | 16% | 13% |
| 40-52 weeks | 21% | 13% | 13% | 24% | 20% | 18% |
| Total | 100% | 100% | 100% | 100% | 100% | 100% |
| Average weeks | 20.1 | 17.5 | 16.1 | 20.1 | 21.1 | 19.0 |
| Median weeks | 14.0 | 12.0 | 9.0 | 12.0 | 16.0 | 12.6 |

*Notes*: N = number of products, which is defined as a UPC in a given retailer-city.

31

Table 6

**Percent of Widely Available Products, by Minimum Product Availability**

| Available in % of Stores: | Frozen Novelty (N=532) | Pasta (N=968) | Hot Dog (N=386) | Ice Cream (N=965) | Salad Dressing (N=1,024) | Average |
|---|---|---|---|---|---|---|
| **Low Availability:** | | | | | | |
| 0% to 10% | 3% | 1% | 5% | 2% | 2% | 3% |
| 10% to 20% | 2% | 1% | 5% | 2% | 1% | 2% |
| 20% to 30% | 1% | 1% | 2% | 1% | 1% | 1% |
| 30% to 40% | 1% | 1% | 3% | 2% | 1% | 2% |
| 40% to 50% | 6% | 2% | 4% | 4% | 3% | 4% |
| Sub-total | 12% | 7% | 19% | 12% | 8% | 12% |
| **Intermediate Availability:** | | | | | | |
| 50% to 60% | 10% | 7% | 8% | 12% | 9% | 9% |
| 60% to 70% | 20% | 15% | 11% | 18% | 18% | 16% |
| 70% to 80% | 27% | 25% | 24% | 25% | 24% | 25% |
| 80% to 90% | 22% | 28% | 24% | 20% | 24% | 23% |
| Sub-total | 79% | 75% | 66% | 74% | 76% | 74% |
| **Wide Availability:** | | | | | | |
| 90% to 99% | 8% | 16% | 12% | 11% | 12% | 12% |
| >99% | 1% | 2% | 2% | 3% | 4% | 2% |
| Sub-total | 9% | 18% | 15% | 14% | 16% | 14% |

*Notes*: N = number of products, which is defined as a UPC in a given retailer-city. The data sample is restricted to products with wide availability, which is defined as median retail distribution of 90% to 100% of stores. Each column sums to 100%.

# Table 7

## RMSE of Log Product Distribution

| RMSE: | Frozen Novelty (N=178) | Pasta (N=349) | Hot Dog (N=91) | Ice Cream (N=336) | Salad Dressing (N=335) | Average |
|---|---|---|---|---|---|---|
| **% of Products** | | | | | | |
| Low Variability: | | | | | | |
| 0% to 5% | 3% | 21% | 24% | 6% | 9% | 13% |
| 5% to 10% | 22% | 36% | 25% | 15% | 18% | 23% |
| Sub-total | 25% | 56% | 49% | 22% | 26% | 36% |
| Intermediate Variability: | | | | | | |
| 10% to 15% | 25% | 19% | 20% | 30% | 21% | 23% |
| 15% to 20% | 16% | 12% | 14% | 19% | 19% | 16% |
| Sub-total | 40% | 31% | 34% | 49% | 39% | 39% |
| High Variability: | | | | | | |
| 20% to 25% | 15% | 8% | 7% | 13% | 15% | 11% |
| >25% | 20% | 5% | 10% | 17% | 20% | 14% |
| Sub-total | 34% | 13% | 16% | 30% | 34% | 26% |
| Mean RMSE | 18% | 11% | 12% | 17% | 17% | 15% |
| Median RMSE | 15% | 9% | 10% | 15% | 16% | 13% |

*Notes*: N = number of products, which is defined as a UPC. The table reports the root mean square error from regressions using log ACV as the dependent variable. A set of retailer-city and time fixed effects are employed, along with a retailer-city specific quadratic time trend. Each column sums to 100%.

# Figure 1

## Histogram of the Cross-Price Elasticity Percent Bias for

## Products in the Hot Dog Category

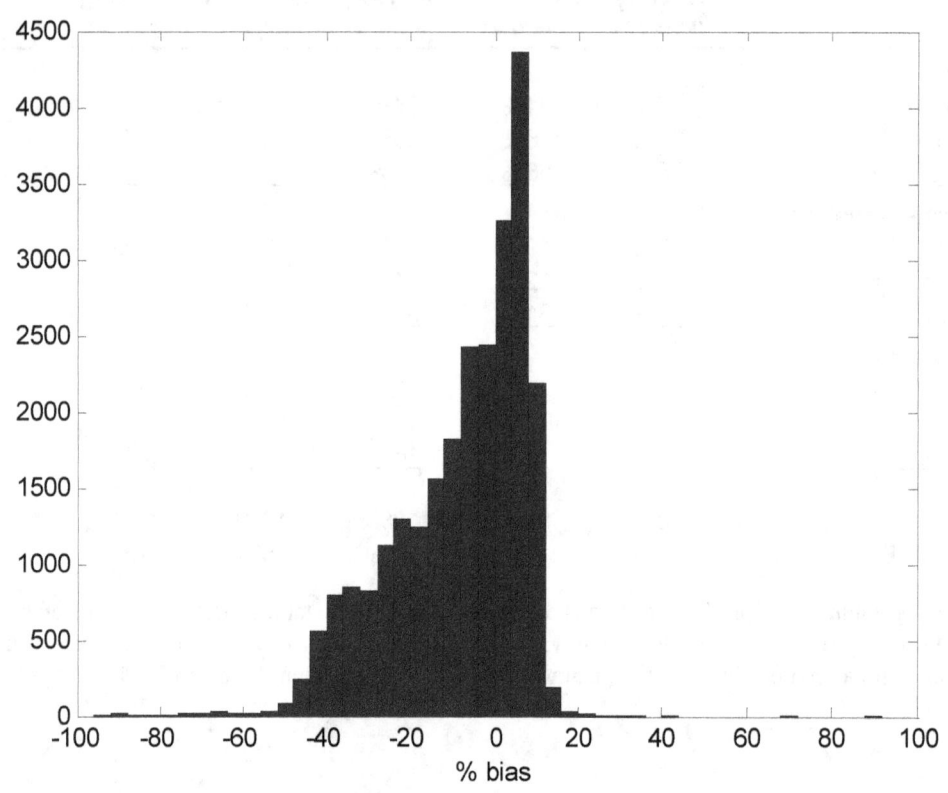

*Notes*: The hot dog category contains 250 UPCs, which results in 25,528 cross-price elasticity pairs. The mean bias is -10.6%, with a standard deviation of 16.1%.

www.ingramcontent.com/pod-product-compliance
Lightning Source LLC
Chambersburg PA
CBHW081243170526
45165CB00009B/3179